THE
INUIT

by Elizabeth Hahn

Illustrated by Luciano Lazzarino

ROURKE PUBLICATIONS, INC.

VERO BEACH, FLORIDA 32964

CONTENTS

Library of Congress Cataloging-in-Publication Data

Hahn, Elizabeth, 1942-
  The Inuit / by Elizabeth Hahn.
    p.   cm. —(Native American people)
  Includes index.
  Summary: Describes the history, culture, and ennvironment of the Eskimos and the many changes brought about by their contact with the "white people's" society.
    1. Eskimos—Juvenile literature. [1. Eskimos. 2. Indians of North America.] I. Title. II. Series.
  E99.E7H2 1990   970.004'971—dc20   90-30780
  ISBN 0-86625-386-6   AC

INTRODUCTION

Inuit is the name the Eskimos prefer to call themselves. It means "the people." Their neighboring native Americans in North America apparently gave them the name Eskimo, which means "eater of raw meat." It is true that the Inuit ate their meat raw or frozen, but that was because they either had no way — or too slow a way — to cook it, not because they preferred it that way. Much of the rest of the Inuit diet was unusual, too, reflecting life in the harsh, barren North. For example, two special treats for the Inuit were the undigested contents of a caribou's stomach and a soup made from a mixture of water and seal blood. This may sound strange and unappetizing to us, but the Inuit were only making best use of their surroundings. However unusual their diet, they were among the healthiest people in the world.

Today, most scientists believe that these people migrated to North America from central Asia thousands of years ago. The Inuits' light brown skin, straight black hair, dark eyes, and wide faces with high cheek bones were strikingly similar to the Mongoloid peoples' in Asia.

Crossing at the Bering Strait, these Asians settled first along the Alaskan coast where they could hunt both sea and land animals. Some pushed farther into the Canadian Arctic, and others forged their way across the continent as far as Greenland, more than 6,000 miles away. No one is sure why the Inuit chose to settle in this cold and barren area at the top of the world, but they must have been resourceful to overcome the hardships of everyday life there. Their new home, after all, was frozen under ice and snow for nine months of the year. The people needed endurance as well as ingenuity to survive. Quickly, these explorers learned to use everything the land had to offer.

the *Inuit*

NORTH POLE +

15°

ICELAND

Arctic Ocean

165° East Longitude

Bering Sea

Siberian Inuit

GREENLAND (DENMARK)

East Greenland Inuit

Polar Inuit

West Greenland Inuit

Aleuts

Bering Strait Inuit

North Alaskan Inuit

Baffin Bay

ALASKA (U.S.A.)

Igloolik Inuit

45°

South Western Alaskan Inuit

Mackenzie Inuit

Netsilik Inuit

Baffinland Inuit

North Atlantic Ocean

West

Inuit

Copper Inuit

Labrador Coast Inuit

ARCTIC CIRCLE

Sadlirmuit Inuit

Labrador Inuit

Caribou Inuit

60° North Latitude

Hudson Bay

75°

135°

CANADA

105°

History

When the people we know as Eskimos came from Siberia, there may have been a land bridge between the two continents of Asia and North America. Or the two land masses may have been linked together by a solid mass of winter ice. These ancient tribespeople may have discovered Alaska inadvertently by wandering farther and farther eastward across Siberia in search of food. Perhaps they found the hunting so good in Alaska that they decided to stay. A plentiful supply of food would have been reason enough for the migrants to settle in this part of the world. However, hard as it may be to believe, the climate was actually warmer along the Alaskan coast than it was in many of the interior parts of Asia from which these people came! This, too, could have been a reason for their having stayed in the new land.

It is also possible that they ventured too far across the spring ice, which then melted and left only water behind them. If that was the case, they would have been stranded in a strange new land. Either way, the people were totally cut off from other civilizations, so they developed their own unique way of life.

Stone artifacts — tools, for example — that scientists have dated as far back as 4000 B.C. have been found in Alaska. Archaeologists have named this time period the *Arctic Small Tool Tradition*. The presence of such tools indicates that their makers hunted seals along the coast and caribou inland during this time.

Other evidence in northwest Alaska dating from about 1800 B.C. — during a time called the *Old Whaling Period* — also relates to the Inuit. Scientists have

learned that these people had a well-developed sea and land hunting system, and that they lived in semi-subterranean winter dwellings made of logs.

It is easy to see how quickly these people adapted to what they could not change. Vegetables and other plant food, except for the mosses and berries of summer, were nonexistent in this frozen land. For that reason, hunting, mainly in the sea, was the only source of food. Weapons to hunt seals, walruses, polar bears, whales and small fish were made from bone and driftwood. These animals also provided skins for the Inuits' boats, tents, and clothing, and oil for heat, light and cooking.

By the time the Russians discovered Alaska, the Inuit were an independent and self-sufficient group of people. Vitus Bering, a Danish sea captain, had been commissioned by the Russian Czar, Peter the Great, to explore Siberia. In 1723,

Bering first sailed through the strait that later was to be named for him. The fog, however, was so thick that Bering never saw Alaska even though it was just a few miles away. It was not until 1741, when he led a second expedition there, that Bering discovered the new land and the Inuit. He was amazed that the hunting was so bountiful, and he brought many valuable furs back to Russia. Excited by the prospect of great wealth, many Russians set out for Alaska to begin trapping. They soon learned, however, that they needed the expertise and survival tactics of the Inuit if they were to succeed. And the Inuit were happy to exchange their knowledge and their furs for tools, blankets, food, and clothing from the Russian traders.

In 1799, the Russian American Company was established. It ruled Alaska for almost seventy years. A Russian named Alexander Baranof was assigned to run

Vitus Bering.

the company. He forced the Inuit to sell all of their furs only to the Russians. The fur of the sea otter was extremely valuable, and, due to the demand for it, the sea otter population was practically wiped out during these years.

Baranof ruled like a king. He paid very small wages to the Inuit, and punished them severely if they refused to work for him.

The city of Sitka was headquarters for the Russian American Company. Baranof built a huge wooden house there, and the people called it Baranof's castle. When the fur trading business slowed down, in less than a hundred years, the animals became scarce. This, combined with the fact that it was difficult to defend such a remote land, resulted in Russia's decision to sell Alaska to the United States in 1867. Once again, the Inuit were on their own.

Peter the Great.

William H. Seward.

Seward's Folly

In 1866, the Russian American Company offered to sell Alaska to the United States for $7,200,000 — less than 2¢ an acre. No one in the United States was interested. All they could see were the miles and miles of ice and snow there.

One person, however, was very interested. It was the Secretary of State, William H. Seward. Seward, with the help of a powerful friend, Charles Sumner, persuaded Congress that they should buy this land. So, at four o'clock in the morning, March 30, 1867, in Washington, DC, William Seward and Baron Edward de Stoeckl of Russia signed the bill of sale. It had taken them until four o'clock in the morning to come to mutually acceptable wording of the contract.

When the United States citizens woke up later that morning and heard the news, they were outraged. They called the agreement "Seward's Folly," and referred to Alaska as "Seward's Icebox." It did not take long, however, for the United States to earn back that investment many times over. Just a hundred years later, when oil was discovered in Prudhoe Bay, Alaska, the government received more than $9 million in taxes and leases in only one year.

Inuit Society

All social life centered around the family unit, which consisted of a husband, wife, and their children. Marriages were often arranged by parents, but formal marriage ceremonies were rare. Most often, the bride simply moved in with her new husband. Nor was it unusual for parents and grandparents to share the family dwelling. Children were cherished, newborns often being named after a recently departed relative. It was believed that the spirit of the departed one could live on in that way. Sometimes a mother might even talk to her child and call him "father" if she believed her father's spirit lived on in her new son. The Inuit hardly ever punished their children because they were afraid of offending a departed spirit. Children soon learned, though, that life was very hard and that they were expected to begin taking on adult responsibilities at the age of eight.

The Inuit were a nomadic people that tended to travel in small groups of several families. There were perhaps forty to a hundred people in each group. They had no chiefs or written laws. Instead, they governed themselves by codes of conduct that were passed down from one generation to the next. Everyone's primary responsibilities were to help in the struggle to survive and to live peacefully with other members of the group. The Inuit would go to great lengths to avoid aggression within their groups. If someone behaved in a socially unacceptable manner, that person could be challenged to a song of ridicule: People would sing insults at the offender, and the first person to become upset would

9

lose the dispute. A persistent offender could be ostracized or even banished. That was a severe punishment, for no one could survive on his or her own.

The Inuit had very little personal property. What they did have consisted mainly of tools, dogs, clothes, good luck charms, and toys for their children. The land belonged to everyone, and a house belonged to a family only as long as the family occupied it. There was no such thing as selling a house; if one family moved out, another could move right in.

Food was always shared because hunting was so risky. A hunter might be lucky one day, but the next time luck could be with a neighbor instead. Laziness was not tolerated because sharing was essential to everyone's survival. No one would go hungry so long as someone in the group was able to find food.

The Inuit were a social people, and laughter was an important part of their life. They visited with one another often. No one even bothered to knock at a friend's door; visitors just walked right in. In fact, the Inuit did not even have a word for hello.

There was a strict division of labor in each family. Men were hunters and homebuilders. They made boats, sleds, snowshoes, and weapons. The women cooked, made clothing, and raised the children. Mothers nursed their babies and carried them on their backs until the children were three years old. Inuit women also were skilled furriers who could sew furs together so closely that they were watertight.

Mother and child from the Bering Coast.

The Tundra

Home to the Inuit was a lonely, barren land called the *tundra*, a region of tree-less plains that circles the top of the world. The tundra begins where the forests end, and reaches north to the shores of the Arctic Ocean. This region is so close to the top of the world that the sun is never seen high above the horizon — even at noon on a midsummer day. The sun's rays strike the earth at such a low angle that they provide little heat. Winters are long and cold, and the summers short and cool. During the coldest months, the temperature averages between -20° and -30° Fahrenheit, but it has been known to drop as low as -80° Fahrenheit. Winds make it even colder. Snow blankets the country from September to June, and blizzards can force people to stay indoors for days at a time. Ice covers the ocean, lakes, and streams in these winter months.

This region is also called the "Land of the Midnight Sun" because the sun shines all day and night for part of each summer. The opposite is true in winter when the sun does not shine at all for two to three months at a time. Then the only light that people have is a faint glow from the sun as it lies just below the horizon, and the light from the moon and stars as it is reflected off the snow on clear nights.

During the short summer, only the top few inches of the ground thaws. The rest is permanently frozen, hence the name *permafrost*. Shrubs with shallow roots, vines, moss, lichen, and wild flowers grow quickly during this warm season. It is the Inuits' only chance to have fresh berries to vary their diet.

Hunting as a Way of Life

Since the Inuit lived in a snow-covered land where farming was impossible, they had to survive by hunting and fishing. Animals were crucial to the Inuits' survival. They provided materials to make boats, tents, tools, and clothing; oil for heat, light, and cooking; and food to eat. Most Inuit lived near the sea because it was warmer than inland, and the waters provided most of their food. They hunted seals, walruses, polar bears, whales, and fish. During the winter, they lived in snow houses or shelters made of sod, and they traveled over the snow and ice in dogsleds in search of food. In the summer, they lived in animal skin tents and sailed the Arctic waters in animal skin boats. With the help of their

dogs, huskies, the Inuit also became expert hunters.

Hunting provided the only food available for the huskies, too, so the dogs developed a keen nose for sniffing out prey. In winter, one of the most effective ways of hunting seals was to catch these water animals at their breathing holes. Out on the ice fields where there was hardly any open water, the seals needed to maintain a series of holes so that they could regularly surface for air. They used their teeth to gnaw large holes in the ice, but in a very short time, these holes would be covered with a thin layer of ice and snow. The holes were hard to detect visually, but the huskies became good at sniffing them out.

Discovering the seals' breathing holes, however, was only the first part of the hunt. Often a hunter would have to wait patiently at the hole for hours before a seal came for him to harpoon. The hunter would often carve a snow seat for himself, sit down, and place a piece of fur, hair-side up, under his feet to keep warm and comfortable while he waited.

He also inserted a thin ivory rod through the crust of snow covering the hole. The rod would jiggle as the seal approached to surface. Without actually seeing the seal, the hunter would thrust his harpoon into the hole and kill the seal. Then he pulled the dead animal up through the hole, withdrew his harpoon, and closed the wound with small ivory pins so that no more blood could escape. Seal blood was an important food and, sometimes, as a special treat, it was made into a kind of chewing gum for the children.

In winter, the hunters also pushed far out onto the ice in search of polar bears. This was a far more dangerous animal to hunt than the seal. The huskies would track the bear over the pack ice, surround it, and hold it at bay, darting in and out by the bear's feet, at times close enough to nip them. But this was very risky because the bear could easily kill a dog with one swipe of its mighty paw. Its claws could rake like knives through the skin of the husky. The hunt was no less risky for the Inuit who had to get close enough to the bear to spear it. Standing on its back legs, a bear was bigger than a man, and could deliver a killing blow with one of its front paws. Today, a rifle allows the hunter more safety through distance, but hunting bear still can never be considered a risk-free adventure.

Hunting was an easier task in the spring and summer. The seals would

come out of the water to lie on the ice and bask in the sun. They picked an open flat place on the ice so that they could hear or see a bear approaching. Seals were a bear's favorite food. The hunters crawled slowly over the ice until they got close enough to spear the napping seal.

Today, these hunters crawl over the ice, pushing a small white screen in front of them. The screen, resting on a little pair of skis, has a hole in it just big enough for the end of a rifle barrel to poke through. The rifle gives the hunter the advantage of being able to kill his prey from a safer distance.

Summer was also a time when the Inuit could hunt on the open water in their kayaks. A *kayak* was a small boat with space for just one person. It was maneuvered with a long, double paddle.

Individual hunters would harpoon swimming seals from their kayaks. This canoe-like boat moved so quietly that the hunter could come very close to a swimming seal without being heard.

Kayaks were also used to hunt the migrating caribou as they swam across rivers and lakes. The caribou is a reindeer-like animal that migrated in great packs across the tundra in the summer. Caribous' fur coats were at their prime during this season, so the Inuit hunted the animal constantly to store up food and to get enough skin for new winter clothes. The biggest danger of hunting caribou in the open water was that a hunter and his kayak might be crushed as the hunter paddled his way in and out of the swimming herd. The caribou swam so closely together that their massed antlers looked like a forest of bare trees moving over the

water. A hunter could easily get trapped in such a "forest."

Umiaks were larger, animal-skin-covered boats that the Inuit made to hunt whales. An umiak could hold eight to ten men. As soon as a whale was sighted, the men would launch their umiaks from the shore and paddle out in pursuit of the great mammal. The Inuit had developed a special harpoon for whale hunting. The harpoon head would separate from its shaft as it pierced the whale's skin. Three floats made from inflated sealskins were attached to the head by a line. The wounded whale would dive with the floats in tow. The drag from these floats would eventually exhaust the whale. Then, when the whale came to the surface, it was easy for the hunters to thrust a spear into its heart, kill it, and tow it back to shore. News of the catch spread fast. Men, women, and children raced to the shore to help cut up the whale and carry it back to their camp. As they worked, the people stuffed their cheeks full of the delicious blubber. Whale skin, too, was one of their favorite foods.

The Inuit did not eat three times a day or at any set hour. They ate when they were hungry or when they had time. But after a successful hunt, they made time for a feast, and ate until it was impossible to eat another bite. It was not abnormal for one person to eat five or six pounds of meat at one sitting.

The huskies would stuff themselves in the same way and then collapse on their backs, unable to move. Life in this desolate land was so risky that the people, as well as their dogs, ate every morsel they could while they had it. No one knew when the next meal would come.

Returning from a seal hunt in the Bering Coast.

Transportation

Inuit life was nomadic. The Inuit were often on the move daily — during the winter months, to search for food; and, seasonally, to move their camps to better hunting grounds.

In the summer, the Inuit relied on two kinds of boats for transportation: The kayak and the umiak. The kayak, small and covered with sealskins, was built for one person who slid into the boat through a tight-fitting hole at the top. Around this opening was a slightly raised edge so that the man could fasten his waterproof coat right to the boat. This way man and boat were one waterproof unit. That was an important feature because a kayak could capsize easily. The person inside, however, could use a double paddle to quickly turn the boat

right-side-up. The passenger would be completely dry except for his face. Because kayaks were quiet and highly maneuverable, they made excellent hunting vehicles.

The umiak was a larger, open boat covered with animal skins. It was used to carry big loads: An entire family or a two-ton load of blubber. The average length of an umiak was thirty-five to forty feet. But in spite of its size, it was light enough for two men to carry.

Perhaps the Inuits' best known means of transportation was the dogsled, or *komatik*. It was an adaptation of the Siberian reindeer sled. Constructed from driftwood and cross pieces of whale bone, the komatik had a light but sturdy frame that was set on runners made of wood or ivory walrus tusks. Before setting out on a trip, the Inuit poured water over the sled's runners. The water would freeze instantly, allowing the runners to glide more easily.

The sleds were pulled by husky dogs, who were valued for their stamina and endurance. Even when the going was tough and food was scarce, huskies could continue to work until they dropped. The huskies, hitched to the sleds in teams of seven to fourteen dogs, could each pull a hundred or more pounds.

Two kinds of hitches were used for the dogs. The Nome hitch positioned one dog in front as the leader. Behind it, the other dogs were paired in a double line.

When the terrain was particularly rough, the fan hitch made the going easier for the dogs. Each dog was on a separate tow line, so they all could spread out like a fan in front of the sled.

On steep downhill courses, the dogs were tied to the back of the sled to keep it from going too fast.

After a long day on the snow and ice, the dogs were tethered outside the hunters' shelter to rest. Huskies always slept outside even when the temperatures hovered as low as -60° Fahrenheit. Lying down, they curled up with their noses tucked under their tails. Their thick fur protected them from the frigid cold. During the night, they often were covered with a thin layer of snow, which made them look like miniature igloos. But this snow gave them added insulation against the cold. In the morning, the snowy mounds would wriggle and erupt into miniature blizzards as the dogs cracked their way out of their snow shells and shook themselves off.

(Photo courtesy of Anchorage Museum of History and Art)

A village along the Kuskokwim.

(Photo courtesy of Cook Inlet Historical Society)

Sod house, Point Barrow.

The Igloo

When we hear the word igloo, we tend to think only of a snow house, but the word actually meant any dwelling for the Inuit. The Inuit lived in three different kinds of dwellings — sod houses, snow houses, and tents — depending on the season, materials available, and the length of time to be spent in the place. Most dwellings consisted of a single, semi-subterranean room. The dwellings were dome-shaped because a rounded space was easier to heat than a square house with corners that created cold air pockets.

Sod houses were the Inuit's most permanent dwellings. The people first dug a foundation about a foot deep. On this base they then constructed a rough frame using driftwood and whale bone. Sod was piled on the roof and packed against the sides for insulation from the cold. Skylights made from dried and stretched animal guts provided some illumination. The entrance was a low door or tunnel — space big enough for people to get in, but small enough to keep out as much cold air as possible. People could live in their sod houses comfortably until they moved out to the ice fields in search of food, or until the spring thaw turned their floors into mud.

Out on the ice fields, the Inuit constructed houses from blocks of hard-packed snow. A man would hollow out a space of up to about thirty feet in diameter and about two feet in depth. Then, with a long knife made of bone or ivory, he would cut blocks of snow approximately three feet long, one and a half feet wide, and six inches thick. Standing inside the house, he would stack the blocks in continuous circular rows that wound upward in smaller and smaller circles to form the dome-shaped house. To make a skylight, the builder would fit a block of clear ice into the ceiling. At the very last, he would dig his way out to create a tunnel entrance. The tunnel would break the force of the wind and keep precious heat from escaping. The door would be fitted with a piece of caribou hide. One man could make such a shelter in a matter of hours.

Inside, platforms were sculpted out of the snow. These were covered with twigs and caribou fur because the people worked, ate, and slept on the platforms. An oil lamp called a *koodlik* supplied both heat and light.

The Inuit carved koodliks out of stone. Th̲ ... pot that hung over its flame was

used to melt ice and snow to make fresh drinking water. Ocean ice water is too salty to drink.

Sometimes the room would get too hot and the roof would start to melt. Then a family member would have to bundle up and go outside to patch it. If it got too cold inside, someone would go out and pile more snow on the roof and sides of the igloo.

In spring, when the igloo started to melt all over it was time to move into ﹘ were shaped with ﹘ nd covered with caribou ﹘ wild plants and flowers ﹘ n the newly thawed ﹘ g food for the migrating ﹘ it hunted constantly ﹘ r got warm and the days ﹘ with long hours of sun- ﹘ tant in the spring, game ﹘ y caribou skins were needed for many purposes, including making new clothes for the whole family.

Three Eskimos clown for the camera. The man on the right carries baleen from a bowhead whale.

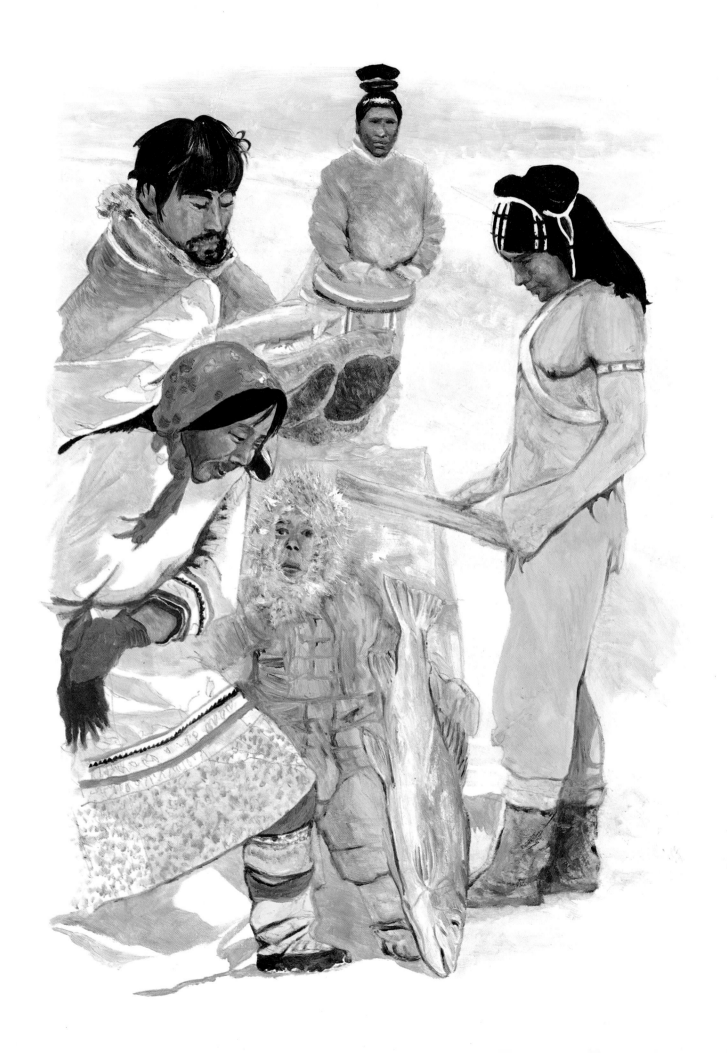

Three men wear the warm clothing necessary for this climate. Note the "double thumb" gloves.

Clothing

Caribou skins made the best clothes because they were warm and light-weight, but many other skins, such as seals' and polar bears', were also used to make clothing.

A typical outfit for men, women, and children alike consisted of a coat, trousers, stockings, and shoes or boots. In the winter, two of each of these garments were worn. The inner layer was worn with the fur against the skin, and the outer layer with the fur facing out. The skins helped to hold the body heat in and keep the freezing Arctic winds out. The air trapped between the two layers acted like an extra insulator. A mother's hooded coat was large enough to cover the baby she carried on her back.

Boots were made from seal skins because they were the most waterproof. Even mittens were made of fur, and sometimes they had two thumbs. That way, if one side got wet, the person could turn the mitten around without taking it off his or her hand.

The Inuit wore special goggles made of wood or bone to reduce the blinding glare of the sunlight on the snow. The goggles had narrow slits or tiny holes through which a person could see.

Inuit women had little cooking and housecleaning to do, so they spent most of their time sewing new clothes and repairing old ones. To prepare new skins for sewing, the women would first rub the skins briskly with snow and ice. Then they would hang them outside to dry. Next, the women would chew the skins to make them soft and flexible. Their needles were hand-carved pieces of ivory; thread was made from animal sinew. Inuit women were expert at their craft. Clothes were watertight and fit perfectly even though the women never used patterns.

The women also sewed little skin shoes for the huskies to protect the dogs' feet from the cold and ice splinters.

Arts and Storytelling

Sewing was not the only art practiced by the Inuit. The men were skilled carvers. For centuries, they had decorated their tools and weapons with beautiful carvings. The art of these ancient sea hunters reached one of its highest levels as far back as about A.D. 100. Today, their twentieth century descendants continue to create beautiful wood and bone ceremonial masks. The long, dark winter nights also provide plenty of time for carving figures of hunters, fishermen, and animals from ivory and soapstone. The best of these sculptures are based on the sense of life that the artists feels in the stone.

The Inuit felt a sense of life in almost everything, and their stories, too, were closely tied to their beliefs. They had no written language, so stories passed by word of mouth from one generation to the next. In that way ancient Inuit beliefs and traditions were kept alive.

Other tales were told purely for entertainment. The Inuit loved to laugh and have fun. They enjoyed singing and telling stories about legendary heroes. Guests were expected to share a good story in return for their host's warm hospitality.

"Dancing on Air" was another popular entertainment. Though it was more of a game than an art form, it, too, required a great deal of skill. On festive occasions, a group of people would gather around a large walrus skin that had hand-holes cut around the edge. While the people held the skin tightly at waist height, someone would jump into the middle of the skin. The people would then toss this person high into the air. As long as the person landed on his or her feet the person was still in the game. Whoever slipped and fell was out. The winner was the person who jumped the highest. Some could go as high as twenty feet!

Another form of Inuit art was the totem pole. The perfect cedar tree was chosen and cut down. The artists hollowed out the inside by burning it — very carefully and slowly. Then they carved heads of animals and birds into the pole. They believed that their carvings represented real animals whose spirits had helped their people. Every totem pole contained a story. Making a totem pole was the Inuit's way of honoring and thanking those spirits.

Whenever a new totem pole was raised, a feast called a potlach was held. There would be singing and dancing and varied contests of strength for entertainment.

The Inuit who held the potlach would often give away his most valuable possessions at the ceremony. These could include his dugout canoe and beautiful blankets. The Tlingit family of Inuit are famous for blankets with unusual designs woven into them. These designs are thought to predate "modern art." Sculptures of carved ivory and jewelry were also given away. The people had a system whereby each of these gifts would one day be returned to the donor with interest. No one ever considered breaking this honor code. If the original donor died, the gift was owed to his heirs. This would assure them of income after his passing. All of these gifts were also expected to be of the highest quality. The Inuit are skilled artisans who have passed their techniques from one generation to the next.

A group of women and children gather to make baskets.

Men dancing in Nome, Alaska.

The Inuit Today

As the Inuit culture became more integrated with the "white people's," much of their old worship of spirits died out. The Inuit were converted to Christianity, and their stories about beasts, birds, and fish with human characteristics became myths and folktales.

Inuit life today is both similar to and very different from what it was in the past. Many of the people have given up their old, sod-covered, driftwood houses to live in modern, low-cost housing provided by the government. Dish antennas bring TV into all the houses, and satellites enable the people to telephone any place in the world. Oil — not from blubber but, rather, from huge oil fields found on the bottom of the ocean — provides the energy for heat and light in each house. In fact, it was the off-shore oil that changed the Inuit's life. In 1968, oil was discovered in Prudhoe Bay on the Arctic shore. The following year, the government received $9 million from the taxes and leases big businesses had to pay for the oil they took from Alaska's ocean waters. The government spent a lot of this money to improve the Inuit's way of life.

Airstrips were built so small planes could fly supplies into the rural areas. This is when the Inuit began to eat more and more store-bought food and to wear the contemporary clothing the planes would carry in. Schools and hospitals were constructed to provide incentive for better learning and good health. Viewed from the air, these settlements still appeared as tiny, isolated dots surrounded by miles of barren snow and ice, but now they had a connection to the outside world.

Many of these things have made the Inuit's life easier, but civilization also has had its drawbacks. The Inuit, for example, had no immunities for white people's diseases. Measles and flu epidemics had a devastating affect in the early part of the 20th century. Many Inuit died in the epidemics. Modern medicine, how-

Seal hunt.

ever, has eliminated the possibility of such killing epidemics in the future.

The Inuit people also seem happy to go to school. Their schools are similar to others around the world regarding what students learn, but the setting is certainly different. Most Inuit children ski or ride on snowmobiles to school. Because the weather is so cold, they receive a good, hot breakfast as soon as they arrive in the morning. Pancakes or French toast are a typical breakfast, served with milk, juice, and sausages.

Children are taught math, history, spelling, reading, and the use of compu-

ters, but the Inuit teachers are also concerned that the young Inuit learn something about their culture and old traditions, including dancing, which was prohibited by the early missionaries because they thought it sinful.

Much of the old life does remain for the Inuit. Every weekend, for example, the children rush out of their classrooms to go hunting and fishing with their families. Snowmobiles have replaced dogsleds, and rifles have replaced harpoons, but the Inuit continue to hunt seal as their ancestors did long ago. Seal blood is still a treat, and the people eat every other part of the seal except for its lungs (which they don't like the flavor of) and the bones. Most boots are factory-made for the Inuit today, but their hand-made sealskin boots are by far the best insulators against the cold.

In the summer months, when there is no school, the people follow their age-old instincts to go out berry picking on the tundra and to follow the fish. They camp beside rivers to fish for salmon and herring. Motorboats have replaced the kayaks to hunt the swimming seal and caribou. Now, instead of eating their entire catch as they used to, the Inuit sell it for money. Unfortunately, today the Inuit have come to depend on things that they need money to buy. Since many cannot find permanent jobs, they try to earn a living from part-time wages. This is not easy because their economy is not as strong as it was in the days of the oil boom. Such unsteady employment can be depressing, and the people are no longer as happy as they were when they knew they could provide for themselves everything they needed to survive. Today, some Inuit are returning to the land permanently to try to find the joy and peace that once was their heritage there.

Important Dates in Inuit History

Thousands of Years Ago	First Asians probably migrate across land bridge to North America.
4000 BC	Stone tools used in Alaska.
1800 BC	Old Whaling Period.
1723	Vitus Bering explores Siberia for Czar Peter the Great of Russia.
1741	Vitus Bering discovers Alaska and the Inuit people.
1799	Russian American Company established in Sitka, Alaska.
1799-1866	Alexander Baranof rules Alaska and Inuit for Russian fur trading business.
1867	Russia sells Alaska to the United States for $7,200,000, less than 2¢ an acre.
Early 20th Century	Severe measles and flu epidemics wipe out many Inuit.
1959	Alaska becomes the 49th state in the United States.
1968	Oil is discovered in Prudhoe Bay, Alaska.

(Photo courtesy of Cook Inlet Historical Society)

INDEX